Self-Care for Boomers

Enjoy health and vitality throughout your life as you enhance your self-care.

Self-care is important for you at every stage of life. As you age, you need to pay even more attention to your health and well-being. There is advice coming from various points of view on different aspects of self-care. This book focuses on the fundamentals.

Consistent practice of simple strategies can improve the way you feel. Tailoring your healthy activities and habits to your interests and lifestyle will produce positive and beneficial results. Simple changes make a difference.

Some Basics:

- For beneficial results, review the simple actions you can take in areas of your life you would like to improve. These include: breathing, relaxation, hydrating, nutrition, exercise, fun, social life, and hobbies. Prioritize your needs and interests.
- Engage your friends and family for support in your healthy habits.

Pick up a copy of this powerful book today and experience the benefits as you engage in positive and healthy behaviors to boost your vitality.

Your Amazing Itty Bitty® Self-Care Book

15 Self-Care Steps For Baby Boomers

Denise Schickel, Ph.D.

Published by Itty Bitty® Publishing
A subsidiary of S & P Productions, Inc.

Copyright © 2019 Denise Schickel, Ph.D.

All rights reserved. No part of this book may be reproduced or transmitted in any form or by any means, electronic, or mechanical, including photocopying, recording or by any information storage and retrieval system, without written permission of the publisher, except for the inclusion of brief quotations in a review.

Printed in the United States of America

Itty Bitty Publishing
311 Main Street, Suite D
El Segundo, CA 90245
(310) 640-8885

ISBN: 978-1-950326-32-7

Dedication

I would like to dedicate this book to my clients, who have supported me in practicing meaningful work; and my friends, who always believed in me when I was in doubt.

"When you take time to replenish your spirit, it allows you to serve others from the overflow. Self-care isn't selfish. You cannot serve from an empty vessel."
~ Eleanor Brownn

Table of Contents

Introduction
- Step 1. The Body
- Step 2. Water
- Step 3. Breathing's Health Benefits
- Step 4. Nutrition
- Step 5. Emotional Needs
- Step 6. Exercise Is Essential For Boomers
- Step 7. Environment
- Step 8. Relationships
- Step 9. To Stay Or To Move
- Step 10. Experience
- Step 11. To Work Or Not To Work
- Step 12. Your Legacy
- Step 13. Dare To Dream – Go Deep
- Step 14. Reflect And Renew
- Step 15. Resources

Introduction

The material in this book is a result of many years of experience, study, observations of and conversations with other individuals, trial and error, and overcoming mistakes and disappointments in the course of the life of the Author. It is meant to suggest and inspire you and stimulate your imagination so that you will experiment and design strategies for your own self-care.

Experiment, try on some of the ideas, if they fit, wear them. If not, let them go.

"To Thine Own Self Be True."

The Self-Care Book

Step 1
Your Body

"The body never lies."
~Martha Graham

It is through your body that you experience your life. The healthier your body the better you will feel.

1. Your body has its own needs and desires. Listen to it.
2. You have a body entrusted to you in this life; it is up to you what you do with it.
3. Everyone ages. You cannot avoid it. You can preserve your body with care.
4. Accept your body as it is.
5. Experience your body from the inside out, not from the outside image in.
6. Your body is home base. Without your body, you are nowhere.

Your Body

"Let the inner god that is in each one of us speak. The temple is your body, and the priest is your heart: it is from here that every awareness must begin."
~Alejandro Jodorowsky

- Your body is your primary vehicle.
- All living organisms grow, bloom, mature, and age. Your body is a living organism.
- Your body transmutes food into energy, and experiences into feelings and thoughts.
- Have fun with your body – through adornment, fashion, movement, and self-expression.
- Your body is an opportunity to express yourself through art.
- Your body connects your spirit to the material world.
- What other people think about your body is not your concern.
- Your body is your own personal action figure.
- What you do with your body is your business.

Step 2
Water

"Thousands have lived without love, not one without water."

~W. H. Auden

The body is made up of 55 – 75% water. Water is essential to health and vitality. It aids in all body and brain functions. Experts recommend you drink between 8 – 10 glasses of water per day. Always drink water before and during exercise.

Substantial benefits of drinking water are:

1. Water reduces fatigue and regulates body temperature.
2. Water helps maintain the balance of bodily fluids, affecting circulation, digestion, absorption, and elimination.
3. Water energizes muscles.
4. Water keeps skin healthy and vibrant.
5. Water facilitates the functioning of all the internal organs.
6. Water enhances mood, energy, and brain function.
7. Water lubricates and cushions joints and protects your spinal cord.

More About Water

> "Drinking water is essential to a healthy lifestyle."
> ~Stephen Curry

There are many methods to increase your water intake.

- Start your day with a glass of water. You can add nutritional value to it.
- Lemon, lime, cucumber, or mint in water provides numerous health benefits.
- Food-grade essential oils add taste and value to water.
- Carry a small water bottle along when you are on the move.
- Get a water filter for your home to have fresh, clean water all the time.
- Eat fruits and vegetables with high water content, like watermelon.
- Staying hydrated in hot weather is essential, be prepared.
- Soaking your body in a hot bath with Epsom salt will relieve muscle soreness.
- If you have access to a steam room, take a steam after exercise, for recovery, and cleansing your skin.

Step 3
Breathing's Health Benefits

> "If I had to limit my advice on healthier living to just one tip, it would be simply to learn how to breathe correctly."
> ~Dr. Andrew Weil

Breathing impacts how you feel and think. Slowing your breathing causes the "relaxation response" having a positive effect on your well-being.

1. Aging can decrease the levels of oxygen in your blood causing low energy and poor health. This can be due to inactivity or poor breathing habits.
2. Different kinds of breathing exercises have been scientifically demonstrated to improve health, support the nervous system and slow the aging process.
3. Slow, steady breathing is calming when you are feeling intense emotions.
4. When under stress, you may hold your breath, increasing your stress.
5. Shallow breathing allows toxins to build up in your lungs. Deep breathing cleans the lungs.

Breathing and Healthy Aging

> "Breathing is central to every aspect of meditation training. It's a wonderful place to focus in training the mind to be calm and concentrated."
> ~Jon Kabat-Zinn

- Breathing is an automatic function. Since you are always breathing you always have the opportunity to bring your awareness to your breath.
- Breathing exercises can be done anywhere, anytime.
- Poor or inadequate breathing patterns may increase the aging process.
- Proper breathing has a positive effect on your physiology and state of mind.
- Deep breathing slows the heart rate and reduces anxiety.
- Deep breathing increases the oxygen flow through the bloodstream, aiding the metabolic process.

Step 4
Nutrition

"The doctor of the future will no longer treat the human frame with drugs, but rather will cure and prevent disease with nutrition."
~Thomas Edison

1. Start with a full physical checkup – find out how healthy you are and if you have any deficiencies that need to be addressed.
2. Address any deficiencies or health issues you may have.
3. Make small changes and integrate them into your life. Better to start small than to do something major and relapse.
4. Get support from your family and friends to make the changes you desire.
5. Proper nutrition is a discovery process. You have to discover what works best for you.
6. You may find it useful to work with a professional nutritionist who can educate you and assist in keeping track of your progress and needs.

The Art of Nutrition

"Healthy nutrition is just as much an art as science. It is important to test and investigate methods and foods in your own laboratory (your body) and observe how various things affect you."
~Mantak Chia

Your body transforms food into living cells. You are what you eat, sort of. Experiment, find out what makes you feel good and what doesn't. It is a very individual process. You must discover what works for you.

- Make it fun, try something new; share meals with friends. Have a party and experiment with new foods.
- Every small success is encouraging. Do what is doable. Recognize your progress; build momentum.
- Drink 8-10 glasses of water daily.
- Best of all, eat a variety of fruits and vegetables.
- If you can't pronounce an ingredient on a label – don't eat it.
- Eat natural food that you cook yourself, organic when possible.

Step 5
Emotional Needs

"Your intellect may be confused, but your emotions will never lie to you."
~Roger Ebert

As you age your emotional needs – activities, friends, habits change. Sometimes you aren't aware of the need for change and continue to engage in activities or with people that used to make you happy, but no longer do.

1. Take an inventory of your life and what you are doing.
2. Keep a journal of your activities for 4 weeks, noting what you do and how you feel during and afterward.
3. Determine which activities no longer make you happy, and, if you are unwilling to eliminate them completely, find a way to modify them so that they now serve you.
4. Take an inventory of your relationships, both old and new. Assess whether or not you need to make changes and if you need to develop some new ones.
5. For more self-understanding, take the Myers-Briggs Personality assessment. https://www.myersbriggs.org/my-mbti-personality-type/

Emotion Exercises

"Gratitude is the healthiest of all human emotions. The more you express gratitude for what you have, the more likely you will have even more to express gratitude for."
~ Zig Ziglar

- Listening to music is a good way to improve your mood and reduce stress.
- Exercise stimulates blood and energy flow, increasing oxygen. Walking is a good, rhythmic exercise that calms your mind and improves your health.
- Slow stretching calms your mind.
- Sharing a meal with friends or family satisfies your social needs and reduces stress.
- Soothing massage reduces stress, improves circulation, and calms your mind.
- Meditating calms your mind and reduces stress.
- By designing positive experiences you create positive emotions; pleasurable activities reduce stress.
- Begin each day with gratitude and appreciate all the good experiences in your life.

Step 6
Exercise is Essential For Boomers

"Physical fitness is not only one of the most important keys to a healthy body, it is the basis of dynamic and creative intellectual activity."
~John F. Kennedy

1. Get a complete physical exam from your medical professionals before you begin a new exercise program.
2. Walking is beneficial for the heart. Go for regular walks with friends.
3. Swimming is an ideal exercise. It is aerobic, involving the entire body.
4. Join a gym or community center that has exercise classes and social support.
5. Watch a YouTube video of exercises you would like to learn and follow along.
6. Try T'ai Chi and/or Qi Gong; Chinese exercises that promote energy flow and vitality through gentle movements.
7. Weight resistance training is important as we age and our muscles lose strength. Working with a trainer ensures proper form and technique.

Exercise

"All truly great thoughts are conceived while walking."
~Friedrich Nietzsche

- The legs are the second heart; the muscles pump the blood back to the heart.
- Exercise improves mental health: it improves mood, relieves stress, alleviates depression and anxiety, improves sleep, and improves memory and thinking skills.
- Consistency is important to achieve results and benefits.
- Find an exercise program that you like, is easy, and do it daily.
- Perform easy stretching exercises in the morning to wake your body up.
- Practice simple stretches in the evening to calm down and quiet the mind before sleep.
- Go for a walk after dinner to aid digestion.

Step 7
Environment

"Yes, your home is your castle, but it is also your identity and your possibility to be open to others."

~David Soul

Your environment – from your living space to your neighborhood – can be an important source of support. According to the principles of Feng Shui, your environment affects all aspects of your life. You can bring harmony into your life by the proper arrangement of your living environment.

1. Organize your home to support you.
2. Eliminate clutter: keep important mementos and eliminate useless items.
3. Organize your belongings according to how often you use them – keep important items handy and available, put other items in storage.
4. You may need to re-purpose your child's room if they have moved away.
5. Use colors and textures to enhance your environment. Create beauty.

Your Environment Exercises

"Ah! There is nothing like staying at home, for real comfort."
~Jane Austen

Your neighborhood is another resource in your lifestyle.

- Participate at the places in your neighborhood that provide activities you enjoy.
- Join a neighborhood watch group, or other community activities.
- Reinforce your neighborhood ties, and make new ones if necessary.
- Volunteer in local activities that you have participated in during your life: school, religious, hobbies, sports, or the arts.
- Update your list of important contacts, family members information, and emergency numbers in a handy place.
- Keep all your important papers together in a protected place.
- Maintain a complete emergency kit.
- Move to a different neighborhood for a more convenient or supportive environment if necessary.

Step 8
Relationships

"The good life is built with good relationships."
~Robert J. Waldinger

Even before you are born you are in a relationship with your parents. Your life is filled with relationships of all kinds, from the superficial to the profound, the mundane to the deeply satisfying. Some have lifelong ties; others are points in time.

1. Your early relationships are generally formed by proximity to your environment – your families and neighbors.
2. Your school, places of worship, community groups, and various activities, determine who your friends and companions become.
3. Your interests, habits, and passions may determine how long some of these relationships last.
4. Some relationships teach you about life; sometimes you are the teacher for others.
5. No matter how different your life may be, as you go through it you have experienced loss and sadness. This can open up your heart.

More About Relationships

"Treasure your relationships, not your possessions."
~Anthony J. D'Angelo

- Relationships are based on mutual trust.
- Some relationships only fit a part of your life, such as a shared interest.
- Some relationships are so solid that they survive time and distance, always returning to their solid foundation.
- Some relationships are so intense they reach deeply into you and permanently change you as a person.
- A relationship that ends abruptly, by separation or death, is painful.
- It is challenging to end a relationship in a way that both people involved are satisfied.
- Relationships can affect your life and your health; choose yours carefully.

Step 9
To Stay Or To Move

"I long, as does every human being,
to be at home wherever I find myself."
~Maya Angelou

1. The life you have built, your family, work, community, creates an identity in which you live and experience yourself.
2. Over time, your identities take root deep within you and stabilize, giving you security and strength.
3. At some point, your life may begin to change.
4. Children grow up and leave home – the house may be too large, you may want to downsize.
5. Moving to a smaller house in the same community involves only downsizing your possessions and finding a suitable place to live.
6. Moving to another house, in a different community involves leaving close relationships behind and forming new relationships in every aspect of your life.

Moving Considerations

"I think it's important to keep moving forward so that the soul can grow."
~ Gauri Khan

- Moving at a later stage in life requires some adjustment.
- Instead of building, you are dismantling your life piece by piece, keeping what is still an essential part of you while eliminating those parts that no longer fit.
- The parts of your life, which have created your life and identity for so long but no longer suit, have to be parted within a satisfactory manner to avoid increasing the feeling of loss.
- You can give possessions to family and friends, or donate to a charity to help others. The mundane can be sold at auction or an estate sale.
- Creating a ritual around the dismantling of one period in your life is beneficial in generating positive feelings and moving forward to a new phase. It is in the spirit of, for everything there is a season.
- Changing locations at a later stage in life involves creating an entirely new community.

Step 10
Experience

"An enormous part of our mature experience cannot not be expressed in words."
~Alfred North Whitehead

Everyone has vast and varied experiences in life. Family lives, work lives, hobbies, and interests; all these experiences have taught important life lessons that you can share with others. Mentoring others also allows you to continue to be involved in activities you enjoy.

1. If you've raised a family and the children are grown and moved away, there are many ways you can stay involved in youth activities.
2. You can volunteer at the school in parent/teacher activities, helping to orient new parents to the school protocol.
3. If you miss the holiday festivities with your family, volunteer to help others.
4. Stay involved in your children's lives in a way that works for everyone.
5. If you have any athletic background you can assist in coaching youth teams.

Experience Exercises

> "Be brave. Take risks.
> Nothing can substitute experience."
> ~Paulo Coelho

- Imagine how you can bring your past enjoyable activities into the present.
- You could start a group with other individuals who have common interests and meet regularly.
- You can resume a creative activity that you set aside while you were raising your family.
- Clean out your attic or basement, see what you find there that you can use.
- Do some traveling that you put off.
- Get involved with other couples at your life stage and share activities.
- Volunteer – if you like animals, at the Humane League; if you like art, at the museum, if you like live productions, at the theatre or symphony. There are many opportunities in every community to stay involved with others and make a difference in people's lives.

Step 11
To Work Or Not To Work.

> "Far and away the best prize that life has to offer is the chance to work hard at work worth doing."
> ~Theodore Roosevelt

If you've had a satisfying career and planned for retirement, you may want to simply enjoy not working and savor your freedom, taking pleasure in your hobbies and interests. You may enjoy working, and choose to continue part-time, or start your own business.

1. When you are young your career may be designed to build the life you want: a family, a home, and a place in the community.
2. As you go through life, and your personal circumstances change, you may want to change your career.
3. Does your work fit who you have become? Have you evolved and have different interests and motivations now? What would you rather be doing?
4. Society is going through rapid technological changes and it is possible now to work in many new ways using your experience and expertise.

Work Exercises

> "It's all about quality of life and finding a happy balance between work and friends and family."
> ~Philip Green

- Work can take many forms.
- If you enjoy working, find a way to continue working with an acceptable schedule. Starting your own business, consultancy, or coaching service may interest you.
- Your lifestyle determines your financial needs, if you need to work and how much.
- Age is an advantage, not a handicap.
- The older you are, the more experiences you have.
- Experience cannot be bought; it has to be earned over time.
- Find satisfaction through sharing your experience with others.

Step 12
Your Legacy

"My legacy is that I stayed on course... from the beginning to the end, because I believed in something inside of me."
~Tina Turner

Everyone wants to be remembered; to leave a mark upon this life, make a contribution. What kind of legacy do you want to leave behind? A material legacy can take many forms: an inheritance for your children, an endowment for a meaningful cause, or a benefaction for a charity.

1. There are innumerable possibilities for a legacy. Start a journal; write down everything in your life that is meaningful to you that you would like to pass on.
2. What legacy would you like to leave for your family?
3. Are you active in your community? Can you build a legacy from that?
4. Do you have artistic work you can donate to a museum or a library?
5. Develop some ideas and meet with an attorney to develop a plan to structure your legacy.

Legacy Considerations

"By three methods we may learn wisdom: first, by reflection, which is noblest; second, by imitation, which is easiest; and third by experience, which is the bitterest."
~Confucius

- A legacy arises from the life you have lead, your character.
- What message do you want to share?
- Could you write a book to pass your ideas on?
- A legacy can be material, such as a foundation or a grant.
- A legacy can be the memory you leave behind.
- A legacy can grow from your life's work.
- Your legacy can carry your work and mission forward and expand its scope.

Step 13
Dare To Dream – Go Deep

"Dare to live the life you have dreamed for yourself. Go forward and make your dreams come true."
~Ralph Waldo Emerson

Everyone has deep desires that may not have become realized. Sometimes you may have a thought – "if I come back in my next life… I would like to"… Some of those dreams may still be lurking in your heart; you can still realize those longings.

1. Get a journal, ask yourself the question – if you could do anything, what would it be? Write whatever comes into your mind, no matter what it is.
2. When you discover something meaningful, ask yourself how you can bring that experience into your life.
3. What would it cost you to include this in your life? What are the benefits, the risks?
4. What are the steps you would need to take to incorporate this in your life? Are you willing to take those actions?

Dream Reflections

> "The biggest adventure you can take is to live the life of your dreams."
> ~Oprah Winfrey

If you cannot fully express this deep desire fantasy into your life because of limitations, how can you participate in satisfying this desire and add richness to your life? (e.g. – you wish you would have become a Veterinarian, it's too late to start a new career, but you can volunteer at the local humane league with the animals and learn new skills there).

- It might be too late to become an Olympic swimmer, but that doesn't mean you can't swim laps and experience the physical pleasure of being in the water.
- Find a way to participate in satisfying your deep desires through volunteering, mentoring, trading (skills), studying (new subjects), or self-expression (the arts). Is it too late to be an opera singer? Perhaps you could join the Church choir, or sing in the chorus in theatre or opera productions.
- Have you had ideas about writing a book? You can still write your book, and find a way to publish it yourself, or through a company.

Step 14
Reflect And Renew

"We all have our time machines. Some take us back; they're called memories. Some take us forward; they're called dreams."
~Jeremy Irons

Everyone has memories of past happiness, and fantasies of future happiness and satisfaction. You can mine these memories and fantasies to bring fresh energy into your present life.

1. Think back on your life – what did you used to do that your enjoyed, that you don't do anymore? How can you continue to do what you enjoyed?
2. What did you want to do that you never had to chance to do?
3. Start a journal with the ideas that arise from these questions.
4. Review your memories, fantasies, goals, and wishes and see which ones are still alive.

Reflection Exercises

> "The past can be used to renew
> the present, not just bury it."
> ~Terry Eagleton

- The ideas that still have life, reflect on them to see which ones are immediate – they have energy and they are things that you could do now or in the near future.
- Prioritize these ideas and goals; analyze what it would take to accomplish them.
- Develop a plan of action for each one.
- Pick the one that has the most juice at the present and start the process of realizing that goal.
- The long-term goals can be organized – when would you want to do them and what would it take to make that happen?
- Decide what steps would be necessary to achieve the long-term goals, and when you would need to begin action steps.
- Considering all the goals and strategies, take the steps that you can take at the rate you can handle them.
- Keep a journal to organize all this material so you don't overlook some important aspects of the process.

Step 15
Resources

"Live as if you were to die tomorrow. Learn as if you were to live forever."
~Mahatma Gandhi

You may want to continue to explore the topic of aging well. There are a few valuable resources that are available and on a national scale.

1. Encore.org – https://encore.org/ A national organization whose motto is: "With decades of productivity ahead, adults 50+ are a growing and renewable resource we can't afford to waste."
2. agewave.com – From Baby Boom to Age Wave. It's "the world's leader in understanding the effects of an aging population in the marketplace, the workplace, and our lives". They are involved in research and consulting, education, and publishing. http://agewave.com/

More Resources

"We now accept the fact that learning is a lifelong process of keeping abreast of change. And the most pressing task is to teach people how to learn."
~Peter Drucker

- Z-Health Education is fitness training supported by the latest discoveries in neuroscience. Dr. Eric Cobb, has hundreds of short videos on youtube.com.
  http://zhealtheducation.com/
- Dr. Andrew Weil, a recognized authority on both Western and Eastern medical practices, provides instruction on correct breathing exercises on YouTube.
- Don't want to explore alone? Meetup.com is a national organization that brings people together who have a common interest.
  https://www.meetup.com/
- Essential oils (Denise Schickel)
  https://www.youngliving.com/vo/#/signup/new-start?sponsorid=23790178&enrollerid=23790178&isocountrycode=US&culture=en-US&type=member

You've finished. Before you go…

Tweet/share that you finished this book.

Please star rate this book.

Reviews are solid gold to writers. Please take a few minutes to give us some itty bitty feedback on this book.

ABOUT THE AUTHOR

Life presents us all with various challenges and opportunities. We can't foresee what life will offer us, but we can prepare ourselves by doing what is in our power, to strengthen ourselves physically and mentally.

My journey to seeking strategies of self-care grew out of stressful periods in my life, during which I felt overwhelmed and vulnerable. My desire to change my life and get back on track led me on a long and winding road through consciousness-raising seminars, alternative health modalities, yoga, meditation, bodywork, and finally, following an inner-directed life path, into meaningful work doing massage therapy. I have continued on to study organizational psychology with the idea to improve the workplace.

Some ideas I explored did not fit; others became incorporated into my life. It's important for you to experiment and explore ideas and practices to discover what strategies fit your personality. I read books, and took seminars/workshops, to see what resonated with me. Sometimes you learn about yourself by what you don't like, as well as what you do.

I began in high school reading books on psychology, and after traveling around through various other topics have arrived back there again. My endless quest for understanding the mind/body has come full circle, and my goal is to stay as active and healthy as I can to continue on this fascinating odyssey.

If you enjoyed this Itty Bitty® book
you might also like:

- **Your Amazing Itty Bitty® Stress Reduction Book** – Denise Thomson

- **Your Amazing Itty Bitty® Relationships As A Spiritual Practice** – Deborah Gayle

- **Your Amazing Itty Bitty® Heal Your Body Book** – Patricia Garza Pinto

And the many other Itty Bitty® Books available online at
www.ittybittypublishing.com

www.ingramcontent.com/pod-product-compliance
Lightning Source LLC
Chambersburg PA
CBHW061305040426
42444CB00010B/2530